Blue Remembered Star

Also by Bren Booth-Jones

Vertigo to Go
Open Letters to the Sky
As Much Heart as a Vending Machine (co-editor)

Blue Remembered Star

by

Bren Booth-Jones

First published 2024 by The Hedgehog Poetry Press,

5 Coppack House, Churchill Avenue, Clevedon. BS21 6QW

www.hedgehogpress.co.uk

ISBN: 978-1-916830-29-5

Cover photograph © Bren Booth-Jones

For Noortje

Contents

If you're going to play it out of tune,
then play it out of tune properly.

—Mark E Smith

MISSING PARENTHESIS

Before first light

coffee so hot it leaves my tongue furry and white

engine on

then I'm driving madly back

a tiny spider clings to the side mirror like a wobbly star

my love my love

you are the missing parenthesis

missing wing missing bliss

barrier dividing road from cliff

my knuckles are white gripping the wheel

such speed whips predawn fields and farms away

whole cities quiver and vanish in the dark like fish

my longing a comet my plunge a wish

JUPITER

And there's the humour of it.
—Shakespeare

LOVESICK IN THE PARK

We lie in the green, white and rose
tumble of fresh and fragrant snow

of blossoms and cold spring sun.
April in Holland. Fumes and flowers. Liquid light.

Drunken bumble bees drone dizzily.
Systemic cherry blossom downpour, I say.

A disconsolate ant
hikes the hillock of my shin.

Surrounding the greenish lovesick vacuum of this park

the city spills:
systemic neon, chrome sneer, trend

and tumour mutating into
            muzak melting into molten

                miasma melding muddled
                                motes.

The whole goddamn glittering shitshow
we forced the earth to swallow.

McAmsterdam and its million
weed-riddled visitors.

Digits fizzle
in the binary guts of the machine.

That's not what systemic means, you say,
unbuckling your Satanic boots and laying back beside me.

Above us, tree tops writhe in April light.

Above the trees Boeings grope madly through the blue,
deliver raving tourists into red hues and frightful highs.

You smell of white wine and desire.

An ant shoulders a crumb
up the analogy of my ankle.

O little Sisyphus! Must we keep up this systemic shopping?

Little kids nearby on the grass
are absorbed in skywriting.

Their fingers tracing caverns
                    where the ozone used to be

they stitch their hearts into loopy dissolving letters.
A message stretched into airy thinness

that says something like this:

> *Dear Mr. President please*
> *keep our grandkids*
> *a freeze-dried leaf*
>
> *make history believable*

NOTES TOWARD A BILDUNGSROMAN

Cathedrals of cloud flower whitely

into steep blue endlessness

it is spring

I emerge from my seed and unfurl like a spikey sunflower

I declare to my inner selves that I'm pure green fire

I am sprung

I squint into the crystal core of my heroes' poems

to decode the DNA of song

I sing

I swim away from a childhood fear of crosses

I sync my selves to the waves with a charm of

mist dance haiku and moonlight

drench my selves in hibiscus patchouli sandalwood musk

enough musk to wither the tusk off a woolly mammoth

enthusiastic is not the same as desperate

and I'm desperate

shadows stretch out under my eyes

like de-fanged mammoths in black permafrost

I paint my nails iceberg blue and stumble

through the city I see an exposed drain

and gaze deep into its mechanical heart filled with hair

ciggie butts bottles glass and glue

grey ooze flotsam   muzzy gunge

is this what flows beneath the glitz?

pain like a hand pressed against a burning cross

rips through me

a splinter under the fingernail of my mind

I swallow the pins of unlearning everything

but I survive   I fish up

from those depths

some rotten parchments and some vowels

I sprinkle them with glitter and growls

DIDN'T I BLOW YOUR MIND THIS TIME (DIDN'T I)

Didn't I go into parliament to please you? Didn't I toil, till and titter through Twitter in search of a glimmer of better? And didn't the litter on the street of the world's bitterness only thicken? Did I not go down into the mines of pitch black forgetting to chisel a shard of semiprecious vision? And when I scrambled back up into the light with a coal-smeared smile and marketable lightning bolts, wasn't I pelted with cabbages and forced to flee the village in a rabbit cart? So it goes. Didn't I multiply a few cheeseburgers into an empire to wire 5000 cows a minute into a million worldwide mouths? Was it not I who performed as the monochromatic mime to entertain your howling and dictatorial toddlers, I who danced before the pearly gates in nothing but my vegan Doc Martin boots to prove, once and for all, that every poem needs a hero?

NOTES TOWARD A GHOSTWRITTEN MEMOIR

I told you of my dream of the cosy booklined flat above the independent novella press above the bookshop with a bell on the door, beatific tabby cat, ethically sourced coffee.

You said, *Better that we burst that balloon animal sooner. Sorry.* And I said, *When does your motivational speaking tour begin?* But then you said, *You're weaker than a woodpecker with a beak made of poppadoms.*

Our love was a bull writhing in a red flag the size of a small country prone to coups. Dictator of the week. Bad weed. Remember that month we ghost wrote our own memoirs? Remember our truly terrible smoking? Two clumsy poppadom crash test dummies and their deluge of disorders. Frigid fire. Flee.

And yet the half-life of love turned out not to be forever.

I don't know where you are but I hope you belong. I don't know if the wind still blows through you like it blew through me, through we. But I hope you healed. I hope you turned that shattering to song.

SKETCHES FROM A SUNNY HILL OVERLOOKING MY OWN MELTDOWN

But darling is poetry a trick
mirror inside the small intestine
of a hookworm
the shape of an unputdownable question
saying, *Am I entering ellipsis*
while singing hymns in a k hole
in a treehouse sixteen echoes ago?

Well, poetry is sick of painting
the playground blue and yellow
only to roll over and go back to sleep.
Sick of asking if it's yesterday already.
But is poetry beautiful
enough
to haul God from heaven?

Singing, *Look at the state of this
k hole full of bullets and glitter.*
Well, poetry is gentle enough
to wrecking ball the sun.
Pagan enough to make the devil weep.
Singing, *Look at the hook of these hymns.*
Shake the mammoth from centuries of sleep.
Unputdownable echoes.
But darling? *But ghost.*

MARS

She hopes for nothing except fine weather and a resolution.
She wants to end properly, like a good sentence.
—Zadie Smith

SATURDAY MORNING

Awake to the surly bonds of bad sentences
apocalyptic migraine to go

seagulls screaming chainsaw hellos

the national budget blown on beer for a poet
your mood droopy as Proust's moustache
you puked and puked into the urinal again last night
didn't you (didn't I)

now time's sliding syllables remind you
to look inside and squint into the inner distance

but not die of amazement and--*Hey look out, Sonny!*

and nearly crash your red moped this morning

into the canal dank as Friday night piss

and as you stop to catch your breath you see

between telephone wire and tree

a sparkle of rain falling soundlessly through light

PALE TELEGRAM

The moth flutters at my ear

like a finger strumming a pack of cards

the moth is a soft downy rocket

who loops up into the white hot moon of the lamp

and is singed

a tiny but final blitz

o little icarus

even small ambitions

may be fatal

AUGUST IN PARIS (VISITING MUSÉE RODIN)

I

This is just to say
the morning breeze ripples the ratty curtains

oblongs of lemony sunlight fade and brighten and fade
on the wall
a black and white portrait of Truman Capote hangs skew

reddish grease stains in the kitchenette

Capote looking simultaneously ten and forty
while I'm lying in bed reading William Carlos Williams
trying not think about how much this Airbnb costs

the plums-in-the-icebox poem is there of course

the coffee brews

you're out picking up orange juice and croissants

I like it when you sometimes refer to him
as Carlos Williams Carlos

your pale green and white floral dress
shivers on the wall in the breeze

I shiver at the thought of you

a good shiver

II

Capote looks like a very weathered kid
or just a sad brilliant baby-faced alcoholic

I hope today will be sweet
like a juicy bite of those anthologised plums

yesterday was hard and sour
in Ben Lerner's version the speaker snarls
I ate your juicy motherfucking plums

yesterday your past surfaced
suddenly snarling
among the frozen torsion of Rodin's statues
cold marble and warm bronze
agony

but now I'm actually not sure if he used marble at all

but anyway you told me of the time when you were nine
and you opened an old family photo album and
a huge hairy spider ran out and

you screamed so loud it reached
up through twenty years of sediment and slime
and shot out yesterday

shot out of Rodin's twisted forest of bronze torsos

like a bad dream

like vomit

III

We sat there for a long time on a bench among the statues
holding hands

a tourist with a tattooed neck and mustard socks
clicked endless snapshots
of the *Gates of Hell*

a brown bronze maelstrom of battered maladies

his camera sounded like little bugs being squished

IV

You looked at me and said:
Crazy how in hindsight that spider was an omen

V

Darling

this city is built over catacombs
containing ten million cob-webbed skeletons
but up here the sun glitters on the Seine

as if history never happened

the Seine along which you walk singing off-key
clutching a paper bag of astoundingly delicious
but alarmingly unhealthy
pastries

and now I'm not sure eating someone's plums
can be so breezily redeemed

what do you think?
such careless theft
of another's safeguarded sweetness

FRAGMENTS OF SUMMER SLEEPLESSNESS

She remembers being a glaring green-haired teen
3AM Saturdays she'd creep home through the dark garden
so high she worried her scalp might scrape the stars

Sundays she'd role her boulder up the hill to church

even then her belief had one foot in its grave
and the other on a banana peel

she'd reel around a party asking, *What do you make*
(of these shadows)

there was always a reason to cry:
bird with a broken wing

or smile: the glittering syllabi of crystal and kiss

often a storm-coloured bruise on her heart

sometimes a half moon of hope shivered
just below the surface
of her lucent blue sadness

where did she disappear to, that bright lass

her footsteps

swallowed by the sleep-talking sea

left no echo

DARK SIDE OF THE ROOM

I'm coming you're coming I'm swimming you're swinging I'm diving dripping delving deep you're melding merging mashing mesh we're laughing lauding landing lost they're granding demanding handling what who's panning who's banning who's bidding best she's fibbing ribbing riling rasp he's rattling tattling scattering fuck I say I slay I dark I must

MOON

How the elements solidify! —
The moonlight, that chalk cliff
In whose rift we lie.
—Sylvia Plath

THINGAMAJIG

thin /

she's eleven

sat at a rough wooden table

a row of broken periwinkles before her

weeping quietly

the dark green and white sea grinds its teeth

beyond the window

a classroom lesson

greenboard and chalk corrections swirling

unsurfable surface

the summer holiday slams shut

gama //

each periwinkle's a planet

Mommy Daddy and me

missing   arachnoid   fleet

she'd swung so high across their stippled spheres

submarined the swished vacuums

of their inner giggles

in search of friends and freckles

now the horror of boarding school strangles the sun

turns the green sea grey

each periwinkle's a planet   but

they're all so barren now

no life bleats in the bleak papery shards

jig ///

oh these dumb crustacean thingamajigs   she thinks

they'd seemed so tough to me

weather-whittled yes
but withstanding   somehow

the Atlantic's deep seethe

the beady eyes of gulls and hippies

the winter's lashing sleet

but they're really so fragile   *I've come to see*

little old me

so motherless and utterly crushed

by the cuss and careless sweep

of a grieving daddy's hand

by the gavel of his heavy heel

MARGINALIA

Stars spider out in the channels that bank the stack of signs

a lock	irony
a curl	subtext
or wave	metaphor
of Keats's	glow
hair	

ghost-	
written	
moon-	no way
light	

the hero
-ine   hello
returns   motif
to haunt   ghost
mean-   shadow
ing

The heroine channels the wave of spiders or irony returns

THE PRODIGAL SON RETURNS HOME AT SUMMER'S END

and he heads straight to the empty beach
breathes the salty sea air deeply
follows the runic symbols
of the seagulls' claw prints on the sand

these signs whisper him along the deserted coast
whisk him on a briny zephyr
to the hot stillness of the dry dunes
at the back of the beach

here sand drifts under the cobwebbed eaves
of holiday homes
locked up till next summer
or forever

nothing
but a translucent lizard
wrapped around a rusty
door knocker

nothing moves under the sun's muffling late summer heat
dark blue sky yellow dunes faded terracotta roofs
and somewhere out of sight
the sick sweet reek of something rotting

the panoramic white drone
of surf
and this hot rich lonely silence
is what

to him
imagination
felt like as a kid
a quality you could almost taste

now locked up in wan
dusty
photo album
soundlessness

his mother smiles at him then disappears forever
his brother bleeds whitely into fading sepia
a photo overexposed
to time and weather and regret

framed by cheesy seashell mosaics
the quaint names of cottages
grin blindly into the afternoon glare
Endless Summer   Bobby's Rest   Rustic Bliss

and one cabin called Ile Flotante
which sounds like some kind of colonic illness
if you say it
in an unfrench way

now he meanders back
towards the sea's stammering
stanzas
stumbles on a shark egg

a schwa of shell
a bit of driftwood
its edges beaten
into formlessness

a sheath of slime
and the inevitable
smelly
polystyrene islands

bubbling
in the shore's scummy
lisp
shopping bags

needles
coke
bottles
bait

a glossy little bird hops past
twitchy as a teen on speed
returned home too late
too late! too late! too late!

and leaving no impression
on the beach

FOUND HELL (PARADISE LOST REMIX)

Resplendent empress,
tonight I perceive a strange alteration in me.

Tonight, the dripping stars look littered.
Memory embosses the flesh of my heart with questions.

Must I crawl, evermore, the star-powdered exile
of never again?

In the dazzle of dark I dream a fenceless world.

To be always moonstruck.

To no longer seek
a high to famish me of breath.

Imagine you're Eve biting the apple;
now imagine you're the apple between her teeth.

AUTUMN TAKES

Autumn, you syphon summer's green fever
leaving cold red flame in its wake.

Can't you take my darling's pain
and turn it into flow?

Here, take this mirror
I smashed into a million shivers

and make a light show.

Take these rainy eyes at midnight,
the desire to be smoke.

Suck the avalanche into a stone.

SATURN

Let us be clear about how little time is left,
what the avalanche requires of us.
—Dean Young

A WINTER WALK AT DUSK

Thrust close your smile
that we know you, terrible joy.
--Denise Levertov

A mile from here the earth crackles and groans
under the lash of eight lane highways.

Already, investors and hustlers rustle
and scurry in the undergrowth along this country lane.

But the cold air smells of moss
and wood smoke.

Rumours of sun fade
in the bare and shadowy

calligraphy
of trees.

Cloud castles overhead erupt into mottled pink
and mauve mammoths. Then drain into dissolving dusk.

Twilight. A lithe cipher of high pale moon appears.
Out of nowhere, a terrible joy rises.

Birds converge and then starburst beyond the trees
and scatter over the darkening river.

When will these silky feathered comets
head south? Isn't it too late? The bright malarial gate

of the equator smelted shut. Or do they live like me
so deep in my flock of delusions, mistaking

north for south, pills for peace, litter
for lizards, bullets for bees?

I look around, dismayed:
the joy has fled without a trace.

But I've no little horse to give his bells a shake.
The muddy path alone awaits, blurry with dark.

But then a tiny bird breaks off from the rest,
like a deviant parenthesis

swoops straight at me and plunges
through my eye and bursts

into a torrent of dark glowing song
in my head

singing,
Give up looking for signs

give up! give up! give up!
and you'll learn to navigate by touch.

BUTTERFLY

--In loving memory of Randa Stortelder

Not all images are as sad
as the cancer patient writing a goodbye letter to her kids

or Hemingway's infamous *baby shoes for sale never used*

or the wilted flowers fixed to the bridge

petals crumble to dust
and are replaced each year on the same day
the phone rang and tore the world in two

a splash of pink on cold steel
the smell of petrol

an amaryllis strapped in place
with a shoelace and a whip-lashed heart

but not all images of bridges are endings: a man turns back
from the dizzy brink
and shuffles into the battered metal shell of his car

away from the railing and the yawning gape
above the overpass

to try one last time
to crawl through the crack of light
in the wall of massive dark

You carried me when I couldn't walk, the mother writes
The bridge inside you is your heart, she writes

and the words scorch his mind

while a little further down the street
someone's shoved crutches into a bin
who doesn't need them anymore

someone in ecstasy is using her feet

the same ten toes it is true
we stand around on serving cocktails to the rich

the same feet we stand around on at our mother's wake

but one day we'll use them to leap again

laughing into waves

BLACK CABBAGES PLANTED

Have you ever spent all night reading and rereading the same five damn lines? The letters like spider legs stuck on ice. Snow falling outside, clotting in the seams of the street. Reading and rereading. Dead flies in a glass. Thinking hurts. Reading and rereading the same five damn flies. It's getting spliced. *How dare you Daddy's dead Eddie's left another line.* It's getting hurt. Damn. Planted like row upon row of deadly magical black cabbages in a field of snow. Eddie's right. Spider's legs like endless hurt. Clotting lines. Ever night. *Daddy's glass--*

SNOW ANGELS

In hospital carparks frozen playgrounds battlefields

lonely snow angels whisper songs of smoke

of warped paw prints in otherwise depthless white

of shadow's shadows

of blue remembered stars

of laughter locked in darkest frost

but then their chorus begins:

this deep freeze darling will not, they sing

will not will not will not

hold back the volta of spring

and birds' green voices

will emerge again

will someday my love

will someday soon

reignite the sun

(F)index

I'm driving a tiny spider in liquid light.

I'm a spikey crystal song
of ghostwritten love.

Remember the shivering syllabi
of white hot moon?

The endless snapshots of the swished vacuums?

The panoramic malarial drone
of Keats's hair.

But let us be clear: rumours of sleet
are replaced each year
in the avalanche of wobbly stars.

But the bridge inside you
remains your heart.

ACKNOWLEDGMENTS

A million sunny days and cold beers for Mark Davidson, the editor extraordinaire of The Hedgehog Poetry Press, for making not one not two but THREE of my dreams a reality.

Love and endless love for Noortje, Nikki and Matt, Mom and Dad, the Stortelders, Jamie, the Boothies, Sarah Manyika, Alice Florence Orr, and all my legendary friends.

Huge hugs and a thousand sparkling high fives to the editors of the following publications where some of these poems first appeared in earlier forms:

Amaryllis, Bosphorus Review of Books, Lean and Loafe, Outcast.
Cover design by Noortje Stortelder
"Didn't I Blow Your Mind this Time (Didn't I)" borrows rhetoric and content from the 18th century playwright Arthur Murphy.
"August in Paris (visiting Musée Rodin)" borrows a line from Ben Lerner's book *The Lichtenberg Figures* (Copper Canyon Press, 2004).
"Found Hell (Paradise Lost Remix)" is composed of fragments borrowed, spliced and remixed from John Milton's 1667 poem *Paradise Lost.* The final stanza is inspired by Dean Young's poem "Static City".